10 WAYS TO GROW YOUR MEDICAL PRACTICE IN THE NEW AGE OF MARKETING

Proven, Tested Marketing and Sales Strategies for Medical Professionals.

Oguz Konar

INCLUDES 3 BONUS MATERIALS

10 WAYS TO GROW YOUR PRACTICE IN THE NEW AGE OF MARKETING

BY

OGUZ KONAR

2013

© 2013 All rights reserved.

No part of this publication may be reproduced or transmitted in any form or by any means, mechanical or electronic, including photocopying and recording, or by any information storage and retrieval system, without permission in writing from the authors (except by a reviewer, who may quote brief passages and/ or show brief video clips in a review.) Disclaimer: No portion of this material is intended to offer legal, medical, personal or financial advice. We've taken every effort to ensure we accurately represent these strategies and their potential to help you grow your business. However, we do not purport this as a "get rich scheme" and there is no guarantee that you will earn any money using the content, strategies or techniques displayed here. Nothing in this presentation is a promise or guarantee of earnings. The content, case studies and examples shared in this book do not in any way represent the "average" or "typical" member experience. In fact, as with any product or service, we know that some members purchase our systems and never use them, and therefore get no results from their membership whatsoever. You should assume that you will obtain no results with this program. Therefore, the member case studies we are sharing can neither represent nor guarantee the current or future experience of other past, current or future members. Rather, these member case studies represent what is possible with our system. Each of these unique case studies, and any and all results reported in these case studies by individual members, are the culmination of numerous variable, many of which we cannot control, including pricing, target market conditions, product/ service quality, offer, customer service, personal initiative, and countless other tangible and intangible factors. Your level of success in attaining similar results is dependent upon a number of factors including your skill, knowledge, ability, connections, dedication, business savvy, business focus, business goals, and financial situation. Because these factors differ according to individuals, we cannot guarantee your success, income level, or ability to earn revenue. You alone are responsible for your actions and results in life and business, and by your use of these materials, you agree not to attempt to hold us liable for any of your decisions, actions or results, at any time, under any circumstance. The information contained herein cannot replace or substitute for the services of trained professionals in any field, including, but not limited to, financial or legal matters. Under no circumstances, including but not limited to negligence, will Oguz Konar or any of its representatives or contractors be liable for any special or consequential damages that result from the use of, or the inability to use, the materials, information, or success strategies communicated through these materials, or any services following these materials, even if advised of the possibility of such damages.

DEDICATION

To Those Who Have Always Dreamed of Leaving a Legacy Through Their Expertise And Had the Wisdom to See Things Not As They Are But As They Can Be For The Better Of The World.

"Life Begins At The End Of Your Comfort Zone."

--NEAL DONALD WALSH

TABLE OF CONTENTS

Introduction

Step 1: Let's bust your myths about sales and marketing
    What makes the world move?
    Sales redefined
    Marketing redefined
    Become the super star of your practice

Step 2: Start with the "End" in mind
    Determine your "targeted" and "calculated" end result
    Reverse engineering
    Your mindset for success

Step 3: Know thy business
    What business are you in?
    How much do your patients know about you?
    What problem do you solve for them?

Step 4: Ideal patient
    Define your golden patient
    Your most profitable offer
    Focus on the gold.

Step 5: Turn your staff into your sales genie
    Sales force within
    Create the script
    Measure your numbers

Step 6: Turn your office into your marketing machine
    Power of video marketing
    Your own Super Bowl ad
    21 minutes of "YOU" marketing
    Ready for true transformation?

Step 7: Claim your MONEY
    How to close the sale
    Measure your progress
    Pack your office with patients

Step 8: Turn your expertise into a product
    Diversify your income

Leave a legacy
Grow beyond your practice
Upgrade to celebrity status

Step 9: Fundamentals still work
Networking made easy
Your 2 minute speech
30 second intro
Online marketing

Step 10: Tools of the new age of marketing
Social Media Optimization (Facebook, Twitter, LinkedIn etc.)
Offer more of you to your patients with less time
Make the perfect offer
Auto responders, Text messages, Postcards, Voice mail and more.

In Closing: 3 Bonus Materials to Change Your Life and Your practice.
Script for creating your 30 second intro or elevator speech for super easy networking
Step by step formula for successful video marketing
Fail proof guide to determine your ideal and most profitable patient

INTRODUCTION

Why are we talking about sales anyways? What does this have to with what you do? You don't really sell anything after all. People who like to see you can make an appointment and come see you. Your industry works with word of mouth marketing, and most patients choose doctors based on their insurance or geography. It's that simple....Or is it really? If you are reading this book, I am assuming that you believe you need to do something to take your business to the next level. Either you are struggling to keep a constant stream of patients or you have reached a plateau and are wondering what the next step should be. And it's my promise to prove to you that if you invest your time into these steps and apply them, you will experience a new future for yourself and your business.

In the past couple of years marketing has changed dramatically, no matter what industry you are in. However, if you are a professional in the medical industry, marketing is just one facet of this change. You also have to deal with the shift that the medical industry is going through with the new Obama care plan, and that's another side of the story. The side that I want to focus on is that no matter what kind of shift this industry goes through there has always been a need for the most up to date marketing strategies to help your practice flourish financially and keep that momentum for the long term. Well... the good news is that all those strategies you need to pack your office constantly and grow exponentially is out there on the internet. You can literally find the information with just a click of a mouse and begin applying the principles of the new rules of marketing and sales to your practice in a way that will create your legacy and leave your mark in the industry. The not-so-good news is that all those strategies are available on the internet. Conundrum, isn't it? In other words we live in an age in which, it's not the lack of information that is our problem; it's that there is so much of it. The problem is two-fold. One is that you neither have the time or the correct strategy to sort the information and figure out what is a credible source and what's not, for your purposes. The second is that even if you find the correct information or strategy, how do you create a step by step plan to apply what you found to make is useful for you? There are ways for you to grow your practice profitably while not spending more valuable time than you already are.

This book is specially designed for professionals in the medical industry that are having difficulty utilizing the proper sales and marketing strategies to grow their client base and income stream.

As obvious as it may sound, what you need is a continuous flow of patients filling your calendar in order for you to grow your practice. The only way to accomplish that is to make sure that you effectively translate your expertise and know-how into a proven plan and presentation, so when you are face to face with a potential patient, he/she immediately sees what separates you from the millions of other offices that does the "same thing" as you do, in your patients' eyes.

The 10 strategies outlined in this book will bring you up to speed with the modern age of marketing tools that you can start utilizing and help you join the small percentage of players who make it big. And I promise none of these 10 steps will ask you to do something that will make you look like a pushy, snake oil, used car, conceiving, deceiving, and manipulative sales person or marketer.

To the contrary, these strategies will help you show you are more genuine, more transparent side than before, since you will not be learning and applying something that is against your style and personality.

As you might have noticed, there are tons of books out there about sales and marketing. Most of them are designed for people who are already in sales, or thinking about going into sales, or taking their marketing and sales skills to the next level. But when it comes to helping out professionals, such as dentists, physicians, chiropractors, specialty doctors who often struggle with the concept of sales and marketing, and looking for simple, step by step, non-esoteric ways of growing their business, the amount of information is rather convoluted and not clear.

In simple terms, if you hate, or don't understand marketing and sales, but know that your business will not grow without them, this book will show you very simple and proven strategies to help you discover what's already in you and turn it into a sales and marketing machine.

STEP

LET'S BUST YOUR MYTHS ABOUT SALES AND MARKETING...

Wouldn't it be great if you had received a semester of courses such as "how to run small business "," basics of accounting", "marketing and sales", "lead generation" etc. as a part of your curriculum when you were going to medical or dental school? Wouldn't you agree that those would be the greatest sets of skills besides your expertise in your specialty field that would prepare you to be successful in the real world of business?

Knowing what the next step is and having an eye on analyzing what marketing strategies work and what doesn't work would give you an edge. As mentioned earlier the face of marketing has changed tremendously. Back then it was all about word of mouth and marketing was merely putting an ad in the yellow books. There was also local advertising maybe on the radio maybe on TV if you had a serious marketing budget and that would help you grow your practice. Nowadays there is something social media marketing. We all carry smart phones, people use social media, blogs, Google, YouTube and many more resources to get their voices heard as much as they can and as fast as possible. There are also avalanches of information available to anyone almost anywhere around the world.

TOO MUCH INFORMATION CRISIS: that's the main difference between now and the past. Back then information was limited to those who were willing to pay for it. Now information is free for anyone and it is expected that in a couple of years people will have more cell phones than the number of computers in the world.

So this is all good of course. That means people have access to unlimited amounts of information but this creates on the reverse side a problem for professionals since people can reach any kind of information. Our filters grow thicker and thicker when it comes to selecting who we work with, which doctor we chose, which company we interview with, what company to buy goods from.

How does all of these relate to you?! Simple. Anyone who knows how to type can go onto any website and start posting reviews about you and your practice and no one cares about the accuracy and the credibility of the author. Then it all comes down to you being able to clear your name.

For example; there are websites like vitals.com, zocdoc.com (requires membership), and thousands of blog sites. The bottom line is that there are a lot of platforms out there for people to voice their opinions about their experience that they had in your practice. There are massive number of people who make their decisions based on those comments about you.

So you might be growing with word of mouth but if you have a bunch of those negative comments you have to fix it. Luckily there is a system that will help you fight through that and show your clients what you are made of and show your expertise and grow your practice exponentially. We have put together a package a 10 step process. Ten ways that will be easily applicable and take your business from wherever it is right now to the next level and help you make more money, bring in more patients and have patients become your liaison.

So let's go ahead and get the ball rolling with step one.

"I can never sell anything to anybody"

I got news for you. You already have, and not only once, but many, many times before. In fact maybe today you sold something to somebody. Any time you influence somebody's decision to do something, you have sold them on something. It could be the food or a book you recommended to a friend. Maybe you took a couple of minutes to explain to your husband why you need a new dishwasher and ended up getting what you wanted. I can almost hear you say, "well, yes but that's not same as actually selling". If that's your thought process, let's think about what makes it not "selling" in your mind. Let me take a guess. You think that these examples are not the same thing as selling your products or your services because these are the things that you naturally do without really pushing yourself, or trying to be somebody other than yourself, or becoming a threat to the people around you with your closing and sales techniques. Also you are not acting like a pushy sales person, but just sharing your opinion. You do all of these things without getting out of your comfort zone. And in your mind, sales are the opposite of all those things.

You have to be deceiving, manipulative, fake, pushy, what else? You might be someone who has the perception of selling as something not natural.

In fact; you don't have to be any of those things to sell and market your products or your services. But before we get into how to do that, let's take some baby steps. Can we agree on the fact that no economy will be able to sustain itself and grow without sales and marketing? Having the best product or service doesn't mean anything if you can't find someone who will buy it and invest their hard earned money into it. As a professional in your industry, you put your heart, soul, tears and blood into your education for years, and now you are in business to make it work. Would it be fair to say that throughout those years of grueling schooling, countless hours of study time and your effort to hone your skills to become great at what you do , you have never received a course in sales or in marketing, and had a very limited exposure to what they could mean to your business? In other words, you might truthfully know that you are the best doctor in your city, but if you can't find a way to help people see and experience what you know, help them solve the problem they are having, it doesn't mean a penny. Am I being too harsh? I don't think so. The rules of sales and marketing are universal and they work no matter who you are and what profession you are in. It works like gravity. If you think your practice is not attracting as many patients as it should, maybe it's because the potential patients do not perceive your practice the same way as you perceive it. One thing I will keep touching on is the concept of perception. I am a big believer of the idea that **"perception is reality".** Whether you perceive something to be real or not, you are right. If you think, sales is evil, you probably are right in your own world. If you think your business can do OK without selling and marketing, again you might be right until the universal principles overrun your belief. That's why it's one the primary purposes of this book to help you identify and bust out your sales and marketing myths. Unless you identify the myths you have about selling/marketing, we will not be able to take the next step. There are very common ones, but I'd like you to find your own myths, and we will bust them.

Here are a couple of them:

I didn't go to medical school to be a sales person.

I don't want to be perceived as used car salesman.

Marketing wouldn't apply to my practice.

I don't have time to learn all the pieces of marketing to make it work for me and it would cost a fortune to hire a marketing company.

Do any of the above statements sound familiar? Even though many people might not consciously say these things, but subconsciously, these thoughts are weaved into their belief system. People who arm themselves with the latest marketing and sales strategies are always a couple of steps more ahead of the game than those simple ignore them.

"I didn't go to medical school to be salesperson.":

As a medical professional, I am guessing that you interact with sales people on a daily basis. Pharmaceutical sales reps, dental reps, reps who are selling you supplies, etc etc. And when I suggest that you to learn about sales, you might be picturing yourself as one of them trying to pitch your services to your patients. And you might not have very pleasant connotations with this thought. Now think of the sales reps that you really like to interact with. Focus on identifying the characteristics that you like about that person. Do you like him because he's not pushy? Do you like her because she respects your time? Does he have the answers to your questions? Does she actually listen to you? Pleasing personality? Good follow up skills? Trustworthy? Genuine?

Do any of these characteristics resonate with that person? If it does, how are these characteristics different than what the patients look for when they are choosing their doctor who has one of the most important roles for their health? They are not. The qualities we seek form people that we want to trust and interact with are very common. Using the right tools, with the right method (sales and marketing) to show those qualities you already possess to your potential customers doesn't make you a used car salesman. It actually makes you someone who looks and finds a way to deliver the good you have to the rest of the world who is in need of it. Put your thoughts into this.

"I don't want to be perceived as a used car salesman"

Think about why people would consider you a used car salesman. What would you need to do for them to consider you that way?

--Push them to buy something they don't need.

--Waste their time.

--Add no value to their life.

--Act on your self-interest first before the patient's

--Disrespect their intelligence.

I cannot put enough emphasis on this. **You are as valuable to your patients as to the size of problem you solve for them.** If you offer a solution to people's problems and you make yourself heard by marketing, not only they don't see you a sleazy sales person, they will be willing to pay large sums of money to acquire your services from you.

With that in mind, I'd like to remind you that no matter what sales strategies you know, unless you earn the trust of your prospect, you will not have a long term sustainable relationship with your client. The more genuine and transparent you are, the less you have to sell. If people begin to feel that you are acting only on your own self interest, and trying to force your products or services on them, then their thick walls of defense comes up, and everything becomes an objection for them to not to buy from you.

"Marketing wouldn't apply to my practice."

No matter what business you are in, if you are not promoting your business and constantly seeking new ways to innovate yourself to attract more customers, you are destined to fail. The properly applied basics of marketing works like gravity. It works all the time. It cannot, not work. That's its main function. And when you understand what it could do for your business, it gives you power.

---Just one great idea can completely revolutionize your life----

Earl Nightingale

STEP 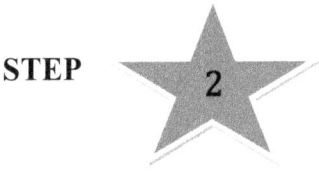

YOUR MINDSET; WHAT IS YOUR END RESULT?

STARTING WITH THE END IN MIND

It's said that before each swing, Tiger Woods visualizes the ball rolling into the hole and adjusts his swing based on that mental picture. Apparently it has been working well for him. Maybe what drove you to finish school and join the ranks professionals in the medical industry was the fact that you have pictured yourself as a doctor, dentist, chiropractor, therapist, nurse etc. But what I know is that whether consciously or unconsciously you have used this technique in your life many times. What exactly is this technique? We can dive deep into how this technique helps you get to where you want to get to in your personal life. It works by seeing yourself in your mind's mirror as if you are already there and carry those emotions and actions every day until you actually become what you visualize. But that's not the main focus of this book, and there are many books and better teachers on this topic. I am using this technique in the frame of reference of marketing and sales for your practice. In order for any marketing effort to be effective, and productive, it must have an end result you would like to accomplish. You don't start spending time and money for marketing then try to determine what you'd like to accomplish with your effort. As they say, if you don't know your destination, you will never know when you get there.

Why is this a big deal? Most of this book is about the techniques and the strategies that the successful entrepreneurs have been using to grow their businesses and increase their impact. However this chapter is about your mindset. If you don't determine what you'd like to learn from this book and create a game plan you will follow up based on the principles presented here, most likely you will not follow along with them.

Please take a moment now and think about where you want your practice to be a year from now.

Taking you time and answering the 2 questions below as straight forward as possible will help you get the best out of this book. Again, marketing without a plan is like shooting at a target you don't' see. And this activity will help you determine that plan.

1.) What do you desire to get from your marketing and sales efforts, if you have any?

For example;

Do you want to increase your daily patient number from 10 to 27 on average?

Do you want to increase the sales of your most profitable product by 40%?

Do you want to be able to open your second or third practice?

_____

_____

_____

_____

_____

_____

_____

_____

_____

2.) If you determined what you'd like to accomplish by the end of 12 months from now, what would need to happen for you to reach that end result?

-
_____

_____

_____

_____

_____

_____

_____

When you put real thought into these two questions they aren't really as simple questions as them seem, are they?

Don't worry if you couldn't come up with a satisfying answer to the second question. That's the purpose of it. Since now we planted a question that is begging for an answer in your mind, throughout the book, you will look for answers to help you get where you are aiming to get. You will find your answers as you are going through different marketing strategies in this book..

This is called **"reverse engineering".** Now that you know where you want your marketing to take you, it's just a matter looking at the final picture and chunking it up into smaller actionable goals to help you get there every single day. That's actually one of the key concepts that we help our clients with.

As Tony Robbins says; "Success is 80% psychology and 20% mechanics." If you approach your marketing and sales efforts with this kind of mindset, you make your goals very attainable, but at the same time you make them measurable.

If your marketing efforts are not measurable by the number of new patients, number of your highest profitable product or services sold, what percent of your patients found you through your specific marketing method, what marketing method gives you the most patients with the least amount of expense etc. etc, then you are wasting your time and money.

In the following chapters, we will talk about what measures can be used to get the most out of your money and efforts.

---Understanding is one thing and action is another. You can spend years of understanding your fear of water and still never walk to the edge of the pool and jump in.---

Barbara Sher

STEP

KNOW THY BUSINESS!!!

WHAT BUSINESS ARE YOU IN?

This above question was a very famous question asked by the Harvard professor, Theodore Lewitt in 1960. His theory of "Marketing Myopia" focuses on the narrow one sidedness of many business owners when it comes to looking into their business from the customer's point of view. Most businesses focus on products and services that they offer to their clients, when asked this question instead of focusing on what the clients and patients expect from the business. That's why after every economic crisis or bubble, we witness companies who focus on what they offer to clients, go out of business. And the companies, who focus on what the clients need from them, thrive.

As a small business owner in the healthcare industry, your situation is no different. Knowing your business and understanding what business you truly are in determines whether you are sitting on solid ground or standing in quicksand.

When I ask doctors what business they are in, the most common answers I get are always

"I am in the healthcare field"

"I am in the business of medicine."

"I own 2 dental offices",

"I am a chiropractor for 25 years."

"I am a heart surgeon"

Etc, etc….

Here is the million dollar question. Would any of the above answers make your potential patients choose you over your competition?!!!!!!!!

I didn't think so either.

Let's turn the dial up a notch.

Let's analyze these responses from very successful practices to the same question;

"I am in the business of helping my patients live a long healthy and energetic live."

"I help my patients get to their ideal weight."

"I help my patients keep a healthy heart."

"I am in the business of giving my patients the best simile."

What do you think these responses trigger in the mind of your patients? They trigger;

--additional questions

--awakens curiosity

--admiration in your confidence

--increased interest

The vital question that will bring it all together is **"how would you use this question as a marketing tool?"**

Imagine creating or modifying all of your marketing materials (business cards, brochures, flyers, websites, videos, mission statement etc) based on your answer to this question. You will notice that your patients will see you as a source of health and rejuvenation instead of a place they have to go when they are sick. If you apply this principle to your practice, I can guarantee you that you will attract more and more patients to your practice who are in line with what you stand for.

HOW MUCH DO YOUR PATIENTS KNOW YOU?

When choosing a new medical professional, what people generally do is very predictable. They either ask their friends or family members if they can recommend someone, or they simply go online and type "Find dentists in YOUR TOWN, YOUR STATE" and start looking for their doctor. They try to find things like, attentive manner, short wait time, caring, genuine etc. Then they check to see if their insurance is covered by the office. The final step is to call the office and make the appointment. What if they were able to find out more about your qualities and what you stand for without having to read some reviews about you?

What if there was a way for these people to see your website on the first page of the search results on Google, with a video of you talking about what business you are in???

Any light bulbs on yet? ☺

People are 3 times more likely to click on a link with a video than one without it. I will get in great detail on how to make this happen in Chapter 6.

WHAT PROBLEM ARE YOU SOLVING FOR YOUR PATIENTS?

What is your X factor? What is your competitive edge that separates you from your competition?

If your response is you don't know, and you can't think of any, well… ask your favorite patients. Ask them why they chose you. Ask what separated you from your competition, and they will tell you immediately.

There are 4 steps to determine your x factor.

1.) Write down what makes you an expert in your field.

2.) Think of your favorite clients.

3.) Ask your employees.

4.) Ask your family members and your colleagues and friends who know you well.

---Take your life in your own hands and what happens? A terrible thing: No one to blame. ---
---

Erica Jong.

STEP  4

DEFINE YOUR IDEAL CLIENT

Think of a specific client or a couple of clients, patients etc that you have a special bond with, a client that relies on you without a blink of an eye. And now think about how you formed that relationship and also think why they chose you over your competition.

I can almost guarantee you that once you go through a couple of these, you will begin to see a pattern. Write down what some of the commonalities are with all of them, and there you have you ideal client.

Also, let's reverse this exercise. Think of a client, or a patient that was a pain in the rear end, you truly did not like the experience of serving him/her, and not looking forward to working with clients like them. Also jot down the commonalities.

Now you know what kind of client you would love to keep, and what kind you have no desire to do business with.

And when you are having a meeting with a potential client, watch for the cues to determine what category he/she falls into.

Why do you need to get clear on your ideal client?

Most of the time practice owners gauge their marketing strategies to target anyone and everyone. Because as a professional in the medical industry, they think that their job is to help anyone who walks into their practice, which is true of course. But it cannot be a growth strategy. Whenever I talk to doctors who have been succeeding at a major level, this principle is determining factor of their success. They know their clientele so well, it became second nature. For example; when asked, you should be able to tell the average age, income bracket, female to male ratio, education, lifestyle, geography, authority and trust figures of your patients and the problems that they are looking for a solution for. Sound a bit extreme?? Well… that's what separates a practice that has targeted marketing principles than the one who uses the shotgun approach.

Major corporations spend millions of dollars every year to understand the habits of their target clients, so they can offer solutions that satisfy those needs. If you are not accurate in identifying who your ideal clients are, any marketing message you throw out there will only attract a small percentage of return.

YOU SERVICES CANNOT BE A SOLUTION TO EVERYBODY….

If you act like this, then you will join the crowds of people who believe that marketing doesn't work.

What happens when you determine who your avatar (ideal client) is?

--Something magical; you create your marketing efforts to attract that specific person to your practice, and effectiveness of your marketing doubles and triples.

--Since you understand the needs of your avatar patient so deeply, whatever solutions you offer to them are welcomed and purchased, which makes you look like a true professional, instead of someone who thinks of his own pocket first.

--You are not seen as a used car sales person when you offer them your extra services or products.

--You receive the permission of the patient to charge premium price for your services since they feel like they have found the perfect match for their needs.

--You will not have to worry about people who are choosing you based on their insurance only. Because you will have plenty of people would be willing to pay extra to be seen by you.

How do you determine your ideal client?

I have a step by step guide that works like magic every time a business uses it properly and it works on determining their ideal client. And the good news is that I don't mind sharing it with you. At the end of this book under the bonus section I will be providing you the information that has each specific steps outlined with targeted questions that will give you everything you need to determine your avatar (ideal client).

---The easiest way to get what you want is to help others get what they want. ------

---

Deepak Chopra

STEP

TURN YOUR STAFF INTO YOUR SALES GENIE

Managing a successful and profitable practice can only be accomplished and sustained as a team. You need your staff and yourself to be on the same page. Many times what I witness with great grief is that the doctor only sees his/her staff as employees who work on an hourly rate and have no impact on the direction of the company. As a result, it shouldn't surprise anyone that they act exactly like that. It's a self-fulfilling prophecy.

Once, I had a client who owned an accounting firm in a little town in New Jersey, and the first time I walked into the accountant's office, I thought it was family owned and operated. From the receptionist to the financial advisor they were so welcoming and acting as if they were the owners of the business. When I finally had the opportunity to meet the accountant who informed me that it's not a family owned business and no family members work at the firm. I asked him with great curiosity what his secret was. He said that he treats each team member with great respect and always shares the company goals and direction with them and keeps them responsible for attaining those goals. He also kept investing into his staff who wanted to advance in their careers by helping them with their school tuition and sending them out to self development courses. You would think that they would just take off after their training was over, but they all preferred to stay and serve the company. Each member knew exactly what the mission statement of the company was, what the company stands for and where they will end up in one year to 5 year projections.

How does this apply to your practice?

Each team member should know exactly what the targeted number of patients to be seen a day, and be able to collaborate on how to accomplish that. They should be given a training on all the findings you uncovered on chapter 3 based on the 3 questions.

--What business are you in?

--How much do you patients know you?

--What problem do you solve for them?

They should be held accountable on knowing the answers to these questions and be able to act in an accord with them in their daily tasks and interactions with the patients.

They should know what your highest profitable service or product is and be able to probe the patients to raise the interest in them. They must be kept aware of what the marketing and sales efforts of the office are, the meaning of them and the expectation from them on a weekly meeting. We help our clients set up the content of these meetings and the training modules, therefore the staff doesn't sound like a sales person instead of a genuine server who is acting in favor of the patient by offering them the best solutions.

One of the best ways to earn an employee's full contribution is to treat them like the owners of the business. Holding them accountable on the growth of your office and measuring their progress and results is the key to uncover what areas need more work, and what areas need to be recognized.

Whether you have 1 employee or 15, it's a sure way to get to your goal if you have your team on your side, and not the other way around.

Your receptionist should also be responsible for collecting emails and cell phone numbers. We will talk about the value of that in the last chapter when we talk about auto responders. But what it does is that for each patient, you can link their cell phone number and you have their email which gives you two more ways to connect with that patient. What you are after is that you want to take their word of mouth to the next level. How do you do that? You keep building constant value by connecting with them through text messages, e mails and voice mails. You cannot just offer them value when they are sick and when they need you.

However when they really don't need you but you keep adding value to their life to make their life better healthier and stronger; your receptionist should be taught how to close sales for you. If a patient just came in for cavities at the front, someone should talk to them about teeth whitening. Not because it looks like they need it, but because it is going to bring extra revenue to your company or what I would suggest is go through the upselling items.

Upselling items mean the items that could be seen as a luxury. It is not a need, it's a want. People might need those services as well, though they might be coming to your practice with a pain but you might offer them something that makes more money for you. Maybe it is not covered by the insurance but it is going to make pure profit for you that could be talked about because when you accept the patient into your office, the most amount of time you are going to spend with them is maybe thirty or forty five minutes. It might not be possible for you to cover everything with them but you want to create the environment and atmosphere and experience for the patient. When they walk in they know that they are in good hands and it starts not just with you but with your staff, your receptionist and your nurses. But they need to know what makes money for the practice. You need to practice with them. You have to create a sales pitch for them. They should be taught not to be pushy or anything or nudge anyone to make a decision but informing them will automatically change the mind-set of the patient because they are there because they trust your expertise on this. That is the second most important piece of marketing; using your staff and turning your staff into your sales force.

---Make a true estimate of your own ability, then raise it 10 percent. ---

---

Norman Vincent Peale.

STEP 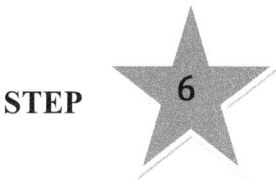

TURN YOUR OFFICE INTO A MARKETING AND SALES MACHINE

Based on a recent study done over 700,000 medical offices, the average time a patient spends in a waiting room is about 21 minutes before seen by the doctor. I think this statistic is vital for the success and longevity of your practice; I would be running down the street and screaming "FREEDOM!!!!!!!", if I were you. I agree that 21 minutes is a long time (Honestly, if I haven't analyzed this scientific research, I'd have guessed the wait time a lot longer than 21 minutes.). I also agree that each practice should work on reducing that time for the greater good of the patient. Those would be the topics of another discussion. However, from a marketing stand point, this research gives you the golden opportunity to keep your practice packed with patients, regardless of the season, type of insurance they have, time of the day, your business location, and all the other things that you think were the cause of slower days.

So let's get to the bottom of it. What is this great idea of mine that would change the way you perceive your waiting room and the wait time for your patients? Well… This is not exactly my idea. This idea has been used by many companies for many years. I just think that applying the same method to a waiting room in a medical or dental facility will change the negative perception of the "waiting" part of your waiting room.

Please read on…

While billion dollar companies, whom you might think shouldn't need to market their brand, spends more than $3M for 30 seconds of marketing their brand and products during a Super Bowl ad. You have 21 gigantic minutes to convey your own sales message to your patients. Having more time to market to your client is not your only advantage. You also are marketing directly to your ideal client, the type of the person who is already at your office and highly interested in knowing how you can help him/her. How do I know that? Well they are in your office for a big reason. They think you can solve the problem they have with your expertise.

Imagine a Super Bowl commercial. It is watched by millions of people for 30 seconds, and most of the people watching might not even be the ideal client for that company or they might not be looking to buy those products. But your case is the total opposite. They are in your office, knowing that they will wait quite a bit before seeing you and since you have to see other patients as well and have to deal with the other intricacies of running your practice, most likely you won't be able to spend as much time as you would like to or they would like you to with them. Or you think you already spend plenty of time with your patients, but you want to multiple your growth efforts without multiplying the time you put into it. Marketing in your own waiting room offers more of you to them. And as said earlier, the patient-doctor relationship is all about trust. What better way is there for your patients to see you on TV telling them more about yourself and how you can help them more with the additional products and services you have or preventative warning, seasonal remedies, etc. etc. ?

So how do you take and manage your waiting room and design it in a way that brings you constant leads, and referrals all the time?

The very first way to do that is looking for ways to add value to you patients' life. Educate your patients even when you're not in that room. You are an expert in your field and know about your industry. Providing tips and clues about how to stay healthy for example and ending the video by recommending your additional services or a product you are selling that will be the ultimate solution for them will not only make you a hero, but will increase your upselling ability quite a bit. Of course there are very vital steps, a method, a strategy to shoot those videos, so not only you create quality content, you also create quality videos. Therefore it needs to be done professionally to have the impact we are talking about. ***As a bonus and to show my appreciation to you for reading this far, I am including a step by***

step guide that shows you how to create the right content for your offer, which will increase your appointment rate and upselling ability. Please see the bonus section at the end of this book.

Video marketing is one of the most amazing marketing tools you can ever create for your office.

I have talked to a bunch of dentists recently and someone was telling me that she paid three thousand dollars to buy a video to be played on the TV screen in the waiting room about preventative tips, and what to use and what not to use, types of adhesives, filling and all that stuff. She was telling me there is no return on investment and the results are not really measurable. While that is correct, what I suggested to her was the same thing that I am going to suggest to you. We live in a day and age that if you watch the commercials or the ads most of the time the people who are on those commercials are the actuals CEO's or the owners of the businesses. They don't use paid actors, actresses as much as before. They, themselves go on TV and talk about what problems they solve for theirs clients. This is a dramatic change. This is one of the changes that took place in the marketing world because marketing is changing from transactional marketing to more of a relationship type of marketing.

People want to know what your message is. People want to know who is delivering and backing up that message. There are so many vague messages out there. When your patients see that it's not coming from the right source (YOU), their thick filters start running and your message is simply not delivered. As I said before, the problem is not the lack of information, the problem is the amount of information we receive. It's simply unlimited. The challenge for the patient is separating the clear message from the static. If you have the CEO, owner of a company delivering the message in person then it grabs the attention of the potential clients, plus it takes your coolness factor to 10 fold. You will be on TV, you will be the SUPER STAR☺. You might not be a multi-million dollars company. Of course you might not have the budget to be on national TV, but what you can do is you can turn your waiting room into a marketing machine for you.

Instead of investing in generic marketing videos or those messages prepared by the drug companies and putting it on TV, why don't you create your own content video and you speak on it? It could be preventative tips. Tips to avoid cavities, it could be seasonal stuff, teeth whitening anything like that if you are a dental office. You deliver the message. There is a specific method that you will have to use in order to comply with the modern age of marketing and HIPAA. We make sure that our clients follow those guidelines to a T. Generally if you are on TV it changes the message dramatically. People pay attention, they watch and listen because you are the reason they are in that waiting room having them see you on TV gives you immediate credibility.

If I am able to convince you at this point that the video marketing for your practice is the next big weapon of today, may I ask you why you would limit that within the walls of your office? How about you take the same videos, create your own YouTube channel and broadcast it to the entire connected universe? Lighbulbs!!!!? ☺ We will talk more about this in the last chapter.

Now one thing I have noticed is that we don't know a lot about the doctors that we choose. Choosing the right doctor for any type of problem is a major concern.

Because there are not many resources they can learn about the doctor's education or what they have accomplished in the past.

You can choose them by the insurance they accept. There are tons of doctors who take the same insurance. You can look at their reviews online but reviews are really limited unless you are in New York and there are fifty-six reviews about a doctor and you can kind of wait and see if they are accurate or not. But there are a lot of good doctors out there. But the problem is that they don't have any marketing budget. They don't know anything about marketing and they are just eliminated from the minds of the patients because they don't see those doctors.

So how you make your voice heard? Simply, by telling your patients who you really are. Have them understand what you past is, your education, what have you accomplished, why people like you and what your other customers and patients tell about you. More on this on the bonus content on video marketing at the end of the book. Trust me. You will appreciate the content you will receive.

I can write a book just on the topic of Video marketing and how much of a competitive edge it will generate for your practice. But time to move on to the next step which makes all of these marketing efforts count. Closing the sale !!!!

---In life, we have either reasons or results….---

Peter McWilliams

STEP

CLAIM YOUR MONEY. ASK FOR THE SALE.....

It happens so many times in the world of sales that, the seller asks for the sales before he or she earns the right to ask for the sale.

If you do a great job of building rapport, sharing your company's story, and most importantly listen to your potential clients and be fully engaged in what they want and what they need, you will not need to be a hard closer. Simply all you have to do is to repeat back to them the key points you gathered from your needs assessment (which is covered on the next page) and read it back to your patients. One by one share with your patients how and why your system creates the perfect solutions for their problems or their well-being.

Think about these questions for a second; do you have the experience? Do you have the confidence to convey to your patients that they are in the best hands, whatever the problem is? Are they are working with someone that is sensitive and who is a true expert in his/her field and knows what he/she is talking about and who by all means does his or her best to help them through that problem? If you give that client that impression then you already know that the flood gates of more and more patients will open.

Needs assessment.

This is the part where you can uncover the real reason why this patient will buy your product/service or why they will not buy it at all. Needs assessment is a method of asking questions that aims to have the prospect talk and openly state the pain he or she is having. Why he is looking for a solution? And most important of all, how he will make a buying decision.

"If you ask the right questions, the person will always tell you how to sell them on your product or services." My first doctor in my life used to say that all the time.

If you ask the right questions, invariably the patient will tell you what they need from you. Because you took time to listen to them, asked probing questions, showed compassion, and offered solutions, at this point you have earned the right to ask for the business. You want to turn them into your raving fans. That is the goal and will ultimately grow your business through different ways and will supply your income and time management, automation, rinse and repeat do it over and over again so you become an expert marketer and you become a professional small business owner where the client see value using your services.

FAQ and SAQ

Jot down what questions your patients ask most of the time. There has got to be a pattern. There is always a pattern in any industry. That is the same thing in the medical industry. You get questions about a common symptom, common diseases or about doctors. Think about all the questions that you have received.

The good thing to do in a marketing environment is to answer those questions before they are raised. In this way you know, even though some people have those questions in their mind, they hesitate to ask. There are a couple of reasons they might think that you are an authority in your field and asking questions might be stupid or they think them and they have been uncertain but they just don't have the courage to ask that question, or some people just internalise and they assume that they know the answer.

But knowing those questions and writing it down and using it as a marketing piece is really, really powerful especially when you are in a sales environment and you are trying to maximise your efforts by persuading this client to use your services. This could be for a specific dental treatment, it could be implants, and if you are a surgeon it could be for a specific surgery. Patients have a lot of different choices and you want to start your sales strategy sales process by telling them what the frequently asked questions are. It can't just be done verbally. It should be on your website. It should be on your marketing pieces that answers those questions about like for example who you are what separates you what your focus is what your mission statement is.

What is your process of handling each patient? What side are you on? Are you a doctor who is beyond prescribing medicine or are you someone who believes in alternative treatment methods or are you someone who is a preventative doctor, dentist or surgeon? Whatever your ultimate set of core principles that separates you from other people, it could be one of the frequently asked questions.

Now a lot of times it will not be that people ask very common frequently asked questions. The reason you are going to make a list of those questions is to turn to them and answer them. But at the end of the day those questions link them to what we call ***Should Ask Questions or SAQ***

Should ask questions are the ones that will give you the opportunity to separate yourself from the competition and give your patient a very clear message of why they need to work with you and why they need to choose you as their doctor, as their dentist, their chiropractor or whatever the situation is that will give you clear message as to the questions that the clients may not be thinking about but when you answer those questions they say uh huh..

For example; a patient is expected to make a decision about taking your treatment or not. It is going to be a treatment that the insurance company is not going to cover and it is going to cost them ten thousand dollars.

The way you handle that for example ; "Mr. or Mrs. Patient; a lot of my patients ask me a couple of questions regarding this procedure and I just took some notes and I have this document that shows the questions that they ask frequently. I want you to go through these questions." You can go through it with the patient if you have time and at the end of that process you say; "You know what? There are patients who ask these questions but they also want to know about these additional things." These additional things are should ask questions. They give you an opportunity to pretty much market yourself. "One of them is that a lot of my patients ask me what separates my treatment from other treatments or a lot of my patients tell me that there are cheaper options out there. What is the difference?" Maybe it is not a question they were thinking about. If they don't make the decision on the spot, they are going to go online and search for the prices and all that stuff so it is going to come up. But when it comes up they are not going to give you a call back and ask you that question most likely. They will make a decision or they will see other people's testimonials online and make a decision and you might end up losing a sale. Why not handle it up front? That should be a "should ask question" and tell them what your difference is and they go WOW. You create the wow factor and they don't think about going online and checking it out and even if they check it; they know the answer. They know why yours is different. They know what kind of pre and post operation treatment that you provide, how you follow up and what your difference is, how you care about the patient and what the recovery period is. You answer all those questions but those are the frequently asked questions but the "should ask questions" are going to help you close the sale. That is the main difference.

Make sure you include testimonials from other patients in your presentations. People love to make buying decision based on how similar people like them with the same problem made the same decision. ***More on the testimonials on the last chapter and on our bonus video marketing guide.***

---Let yourself be silently drawn by the strange pull of what you really love. It will not lead you astray. ---

---

Rumi

STEP

TURN YOUR EXPERTISE INTO A PRODUCT

Marketing has drastically changed over the years. It is really tough to stay on top of it, especially with the growth of the social media. If you're not a part of that, your voice is only heard through your existing clients by word of mouth which could be enough for you, but it's not enough for people who want to multiply their efforts and multiply there income and increase the number of people to help out.

Let's discuss who this is for. This is specifically for anyone who is in the medical field who has expertise. I would say more than 95 percent of you do, and have a strategy to help every client. But you want to turn that into a product, which makes a great impact. This is for people who want to turn their expertise and their knowledge into products and mass distribute in order to leave a legacy. If you have a book out there and/or training CDs, you're pretty much leaving a legacy for the generations to come and everyone can learn from your experience which is key. This is very important for a lot of people including myself. That's why I am writing this book and that's my goal, helping people by sharing my experiences and helping them see the world the way I see it. They might disagree or agree but at the end of the day even if I'm able to teach them just one thing that they did not know before by getting involved with my books and programs, that's that stuff that just gives me ultimate happiness.

I know there are people out there who are in the same mind set as me. That's why this is specifically designed for those kinds of people who want to make a difference, who wants to leave a legacy, who wants to grow their efforts exponentially beyond their practice, who wants to be in a position, who are in line with technology and the marketing and the social media.

Why not create programs? Just take your expertise and create programs that you get paid for and train other medical professionals in the area to show them how you do what you do and while you do that get paid very high sums of money. Because there are people that need your experience. There are a lot of doctors right now starting out not knowing how to start up a practice and they are looking up to those who have successful offices to see how they got to that point. If you have that knowledge, you can share it. I am just giving you an example.

There could be so many different ways to share your experience. But if you are able to put together a program or a product that would share your message with the rest of the world then do it. It could be for the medical community. It could for your patients. Now you're creating a legacy. Imagine having your own book sitting in your office and people walk in and see that actually you did write a book. You have your own book online or wherever that just brings you to another level. That is utilizing the key concepts and principles of marketing. That's what we are after. This means that taking your practice beyond your practice.

You can only see so many patients every day. If you create a product with the knowledge that it can be used by other people throughout the country or throughout the world then you are creating a legacy. You are creating a cash flow. You are creating a product that people can buy without coming to your office. What kinds of products are we talking about?

Let's say you are a dentist. You have been doing this for fifteen years and maybe you have your third office open. You have got it down to a science on how to find the best real estate or office, how do you open up, how much it takes, what kind of equipment you need to buy, how do you get it for a discount etc. These are all of the steps that maybe your colleagues are looking up to you for. That is because you are doing a great job. Why not create a book or a set of CD's, videos showing how that is done? It helps out other people. I am sure there are many doctors, dentist or physicians looking to do what you did. But they don't know where to start.

If you create a guideline and back it up with your own experience and turn it into a product and market it out there, it will create a legacy for you. It will take your name out there. It doesn't have to be CDs. It could be a specific product that you have been using that you created for yourself such as a tool to make the surgery a lot easier. Or maybe make the tooth filling a lot easier.

Nothing happens by coincidence. If you follow certain procedure principles and steps your numbers, your profits, the number of patients that you see will go up tremendously. I am talking about going beyond that creating a legacy. We are talking about creating cash flow that is growing behind your practice. We turn your dream into reality. Turn it into a product, get your name out there and make you a success.

I can almost hear you say; "All of this sounds all good, but how do I do that?"

And my response to that is I don't think it would be fair to get into the ***HOW TO DO THAT*** in this book in respect to staying within the 10 steps outlined since this section by itself is worth writing a book for. Therefore I will leave the details out for another book.

---The only way to enjoy anything in this life is to earn it first. ---

---

Ginger Rogers

STEP  9

NETWORKING FUNDAMENTALS STILL WORK

Networking is important for any profession. It is an excellent way to meet people in related fields to further one's career. Many people do not realize that networking also applies to medical professions, including doctors, dentists and chiropractors, among others. With this being said, many people find it difficult to network, whether it means socializing with a group of strangers in the profession, or marketing oneself online. I will try to explain the wide variety of ways that a medical person can network themselves, and why it is so important in a world where technology is expanding and everyone seems to know each other.

One of the biggest problems that people seem to have with networking face to face would be the issue of "self-image" and "fear". People become scared when faced with social situations that they are unprepared for. This makes the social encounter that much scarier. Additionally, people who are more reserved and are not use to being very social generally have a more difficult time networking than those who are outgoing. A few tips to consider to help face to face networking would be to make sure to step out of your comfort zone. Pushing yourself to try new things can not only make you feel great, but it can further your career. Body language is also important in these situations because having a positive or inviting body language will allow people to feel more comfortable around you, and in turn, people will gravitate toward you. A final tip for traditional networking involves the idea of opportunities, and how it is important to be social and open minded when possible.

Networking can also take place online with the invention of social media. There is a wide variety of social networking sites specifically tailored for the medical professional. Some of these websites include MedXCentral, AllNurses.com and Medical Mingle. Simply communicating on these professional networking sites will help to get your name out there and let people know about the services that you offer. Social networks allow healthcare professionals of all specialties to connect and further engage with the community.

Social networking websites can also be helpful for the medical professional to educate the public about health. Public health is extremely important. In an age where the medical field centers on the patient, now is the perfect time to use social networking websites to your advantage. Other common, yet useful social networking sites include blogs, Facebook and Twitter.

Utilizing social networking websites allow the consumer to create a relationship with the healthcare professional by receiving important information from a professional that they can trust. Fostering this relationship is absolutely crucial in an age where technology is the primary way of communication for almost everyone.

As you can see, there are an endless number of ways for medical professionals to network. Whether it be through traditional face to face networking, or online forms of networking, this form of communication is extremely important. Networking can open up new opportunities for the medical professional while letting everyone know what they are all about.

Speaking in any networking situation whether it is online or at a face to face networking event, if you don't have an exact plan about how you will introduce yourself and make the most of that opportunity, I'd rather you not go to one altogether. Preparation is the key, and knowing how to prepare is golden. Any meeting you get yourself involve with, you should be in total confidence to be able to explain what you do by following the marketing principles to get the attention of the person you are meeting, and attract that person to what you are offering. This is done through a 30 second intro speech or elevator speech. When somebody asks you what you do, you can't afford to mumble and rumble. You should have your elevator speech ready and memorized.

I have put together a template that will help you create your own 30 second elevator speech by just filling in a couple of words, and it will do that magic for you, and it always does.

But in order for it to work, you will have to use it extensively. Although the social media and online marketing emerged and made the greatest impact on marketing, I truly believe that the way to build solid and long term relationships still happens by face to face meetings and networking. Take advantage of the technology at your fingertips, but do not neglect the importance of handshakes.

Your 30 Second Elevator Speech Template is available under the bonus section of this book.

---Our mental attitude is the X factor that determines our fate.---

Dale Carnegie.

STEP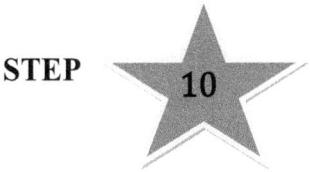

TOOLS OF THE NEW AGE OF MARKETING

In recent years the world has seen an amazing uprising of social media and networking. From Facebook to Twitter, to Youtube, everyone seems to have left a substantial digital footprint. Literally, every industry has reaped the benefits of social media and medical doctors are no exception to this modern rule.

It has now become an undeniable truth that patients have numerous choices in terms of medical doctors. Using the internet, prospective patients can obtain information on nearly every medical doctor in America. Commonly this is done by reading and writing reviews on past experiences and basing choices on other patient perspectives. This doubled with a modern and easy-to-use transit system in most municipalities doctors must be more aware than ever of their online presence and reputation.

It is true that physicians have a unique set of benefits and consequences when it comes to the use of social media and social networking. As they say, "there is such a thing as too much." Playing the appropriate role as a physician online is undoubtedly the most important aspect. Doing something as bold as accepting a Facebook friend-request from a patient would generally be classified as "far too much." However, updating a public profile to help drive awareness and information to current and future patients could potentially set a doctor from the rest of the pack. Using well written and informative information for patients to read and relate to could assist with more appropriately timed appointments and early detection of ailments. Both of these are genuine pluses.

A fitting application for a physician to participate in the modern social media frenzy is simply, a blog. Aggregate important medical news, help patients familiarize themselves with your services and offer very pertinent information on current outbreaks and common community viruses. This will not only help patients indirectly personalize their relationship with their MD but also provide them with accurate information that may pertain to them.

Creating and maintaining a strong relationship with the online community works the same for medical doctors as it would with any other service. In fact, many reputable and successful physicians have found the fine line for appropriately utilizing the online social media tool. With an unprecedented amount of the world's population actively participating in social media it has become imperative for all industries to follow suit. The only separate rule for medical doctors and the rest of the online community is complete discretion and caution to its entire process.

Let's take a closer look at today's media marketing tools;

GROUPON

I know people have mixed feeling about Groupon. Groupon is an online and mobile phenomena that give the consumers an opportunity to get a product or service they want for a cheaper price than the market price. On reverse it gives the business owner the opportunity to market their business on a massive scale through the massive size of mobile and online marketing.

Now I am guessing if you know what Groupon is, you probably have formulated your own opinion of it. I hear a lot of medical professionals especially dentists complaining about the crowd they attract through their ad on Groupon. The chief perception is that people who shop from this site are only looking for cheap deals. They are tire-kickers. They get the cheap deal and they never come back as a long term customer. I will tell you this; yes, you might be right that these people are on that site or they use that app to get those deals for a very cheap price, BUT…. By all means it's not their fault that you COULDN'T upsell them on your other products. Ouch, was it too harsh? Well, there are thousands of sales professionals out on the streets every single day pounding on doors and blasting the phone to get an opportunity to sit across from their ideal client. Their entire goal is to make an appointment with that client. Appointments do not cost anything to the prospect besides their time, but the sales person's strategy is to sell their services at that appointment.

Let's look at your scenario now. You have a client who actually bought a service from you (generally a teeth-whiting session or cosmetic surgery, or varicose vein removal, and eye exam etc. etc.), and that person will be at your office to get the service they purchased, and they walk out without buying anything else from you. Well, what this tells me is that you don't have a marketing/sales system at your office. The good news is that you read the past 9 chapters about how to create that system, so you can take full advantage of these Groupon deals with confidence.

HOW TO BE STICKY----AUTORESPONDERS

Let's just say that a potential patient has visited your website and is interested in your services. He or she completes your online contact form, and will most likely wait hours or days for your email reply or call. If you had custom-designed autoreplies, that potential patient would be turning into a long term patient maybe.

Your office staff collects information from each of your patients on their visit from the medical history to their full contact information and most of the time people have no problem providing that information. They visit you and they leave your office. What would be your strategy to follow up with that patient to get their feedback on the service they just received from you? A phone call? An E mail? A letter? A postcard?

Coming from a strong sales background, one thing I know that works like magic is that "you have to strike when the iron is hot". If you find a way to reach out and get their feedback as soon as they had their experience with you, you will have a very high response rate.

But how do you do that? That's what an auto-responder is. It follows up with the client through e mail or text message or a voicemail with your patient to get their feedback or to give them healthy tips, or reminders.

There are so many companies out there that offer auto-responding services. What this means is that you create an email content or text message content or website content and it is delivered across the whole list that you have (of course you will have to follow HIPAA guidelines). This means that patients with their email addresses will be delivered with content every once in a while regarding what you do for them or with your special campaign or promotion. You don't want people to just come to you when they need you. You have to remind them of your services. In the past if you were able to reach out to people four times through the efforts of marketing it could be online or on TV or telephone generally they would make a buying decision on the fourth choice. Right now with the new age of marketing it takes about sixteen efforts to have somebody commit on buying a product. Why? Because there is an information overload that people have to wade through. There is so much information that it takes time for your message to sink in for the client or patient to separate you from your competition and end up buying from you.

I think that maximizing your marketing efforts through the correct use of autoresponders will make a long term impact on your clients, since 99% of your competition has no idea how to make the best of this system yet. ☺

S.E.O

The third one which has been really famous recently is S.E.O. marketing. This stands for Search Engine Optimization. It is a really cool way of saying that by using specific words there is a way for you to take your company's website onto major search engines, like Google, Yahoo, MSN or Bing's first page or the first couple of pages. When someone is searching for a dentist or a physician in a specific area your name will comes up first with proper SEO placement. This is an amazing marketing tool. Over the past couple of years there has been tons of companies, I am sure you are approached by a couple of them, which claim they will take your company to the first page on Google.

We can write an entire book on how this works and what you should do, which companies actually succeed in doing this, how to choose those companies etc. But I will give you one clue that will carry your page to the very heights of Google and social media. And that is "your video". According to research, people are 3 times more likely to click on a link that has a video than a link without one. If you have your video on your site, it's very likely that you will climb up the Google ladder pretty fast. Again most of your competition has no idea about video marketing. Go back to the chapter on video marketing and analyze the step by step guide you are getting at the end of this book.

YouTube Channel And Social Media

Did you know that YouTube is the 2nd largest search engine on the internet? The number 1 is Google as many of you might have guessed. But the interesting fact is that YouTube is also owned by Google. In other words Google is monopolizing the search engine industry.

Let's look at some hard numbers for a second;

Every month YouTube gets;

--1,586,000 daily website hits

--100 Million Worldwide Daily Video Streams

--64 Million Unique visitors

There is no need to do any further math. If even a tiny bit of that traffic was collected by your YouTube channel, it would be more than enough to quadruple your business.

Wait!! You don't have your own YouTube channel?

Creating a YouTube account and opening your channel is really easy. However what's not so easy is to create and stream quality content so you build your followers. When you think about it, YouTube is nothing more than a meeting place for millions of people every day who are hungry for knowledge or who want to have a good time or who is looking for something. When you have the potential of being watched by that many eyes, you cannot effort to release content that doesn't reflect the quality of yourself or your practice.

Please look into how to create professional content for your YouTube channel, and make sure you have one.

Based on the statistics on digitalbuzzblog.com;

- **1 Million websites have integrated with Facebook**
- **23% of users check Facebook 5 times or more daily**
- **56% of customer tweets are being ignored**
- **34% of marketers have generated leads on Twitter**
- **Google's +1 button is used 5 million times a day**
- **Over 5 million are uploaded to Instagram every hour**
- **80% of Pinterest users are female**
- **1 Million websites have integrated with Facebook**
- **23% of users check Facebook 5 times or more daily**
- **56% of customer tweets are being ignored**
- **34% of marketers have generated leads on Twitter**
- **Google's +1 button is used 5 million times a day**
- **Over 5 million are uploaded to Instagram every hour**
- **80% of Pinterest users are female.**

Creating and managing your social media appearance allows you to be able to reach out to potential clients that you wouldn't have been able to do so without social media.

In Closing: Claim your BONUSES.

I wish you all the delight, joy and excitement of making the impact on this world that is your gift.

BONUS MATERIAL 1:
Script for creating your 30 second intro or elevator speech for super easy networking

To make the best out of this document, I highly suggest that you first work on identifying your ideal client with the help of your other free gift titled "***Fail proof guide to determine your ideal and most profitable patient***". This is important since it is the foundation of an effective intro, whether you are giving that intro verbally, or it appears on a website/about us page etc.

Before I get to some specific suggestions for elevator speeches, I have a particular approach to them that I thought I had better explain so that the examples/suggestions hopefully make sense, and you can make any changes that may be necessary within the same overall template. I've sometimes been accused of over-explaining, so if you would like to scroll straight to the suggestions, please do so!

The elevator speeches with which I will help you with are aimed at grabbing attention immediately. However it isn't just attention from anyone that's important (obviously) but rather attention from the key target audience/ideal clients that you are looking to attract.

You clearly should have a very strong focus on your ideal, although I will dwell on this a little below as it is of such importance to everything that follows, and the power of the elevator speech to grab attention in the first place.

The goal of an elevator speech or introduction is not to sell right off the bat. Rather it is to grab the attention of that IDEAL client or prospect. A great response to an elevator speech would be: "That's interesting, I'd like to hear more about that/tell me more about that". If someone is interacting with you online, a good result is to have them click the "contact us" link on your page.

There are 3 reasons I suggest it is worth spending time getting really clear on the definition of your ideal client:

1. When you identify who you primarily want to work with up front, anyone who fits that definition will immediately be more inclined to listen.

2. Anyone who isn't a good fit for your business, will likely disqualify themselves from following up with you, thereby saving you all time. However, they may still refer you to others they know who may be a better fit for you. I'm assuming that referral is something you are looking to encourage.

3. You will sound different from almost everyone else out there. Most businesses spend more time talking about themselves than about their clients. More on this below. The whole healthcare niche seems to be becoming more and more competitive. Assuming this to be the case, standing out and showing that you REALLY understand the challenges facing the clients that you help, is going to be of critical importance.

Once you have identified the ideal client profile for your business, think about what issues, challenges and problems they are facing, that will be resolved when they work with you. It is critical to retain this focus in what follows.

Most people are primarily concerned about what is going on in their own lives and businesses. That may sound obvious but it is consistently ignored in most elevator speeches. Most introductions concentrate on "WHAT WE DO". In other words they describe the company, where they are located, how long they have been in business, how qualified they are, what great customer service they have, the processes they use to provide their service and so on.

This is the wrong focus to grab attention for a couple of reasons:

1. It sounds the same as everyone else. Giving information about their company is what most businesses do. You cannot afford to assume people will connect what you do with the challenges they are facing – often times they won't.

2. Most of these things are a given – after all, if I choose you I EXPECT you're your expertise is great and that you are qualified to deal with my health issues. Excellent customer service for example, is also the

> minimum I expect, it is not a differentiator.

Bear in mind that your potential patients today are bombarded with sales messages and are pretty adept at filtering them out. Even when they are online searching for your service, they are getting skilled at looking at websites and moving on if the site doesn't connect with them fast. You have around 10 seconds to get their attention both online and off. If the type of business you run is unfamiliar to your prospects, it is especially important that they "get" your value and its purpose, right away.

OK – enough marketing speak;

So, here is the basic structure of an elevator speech that aims to grab attention from your ideal prospects quickly:

"We work (this target market) who has (this problem issue or challenge) and we help them (get this ideal solution)"

You will see from the language that follows, that the most powerful way to connect with a prospect is to use emotion. In other words: how are they feeling when they are dealing with their problems and challenges? People are highly motivated to deal with situations that are uncomfortable, and when they hear their emotions directly articulated, they will certainly give you their attention.

It may seem strange that we are talking about emotion in business; isn't it supposed to be the field of logic? It may be true that the final buying decision is heavily influenced by figures, costs etc. but in the initial phases of grabbing attention, emotion is what will do it – people are attracted to messages that speak to their feelings and emotions.

Using this approach, here is my suggestions to create your own elevator speech:

- *"We work with _____ who want to solve_____ but are constantly frustrated that they are not_____. Some of my patients struggle to_____, others are tired of_____. I work with you to solve _____. I am dedicated to putting in place the means for*

you to achieve _____."

I hope these make sense and are on target for who you are trying to attract. Again, the idea is to get into a conversation at this stage, rather than explain the details of how you do what you do, or go into the processes. There will be plenty of time to go into that when you are talking to them about working together. I have tried to plug into the feelings that your clients have – hence the use of "frustration", "confusion" etc.

Obviously you can tweak the words to make it sound more like you, and you may need to vary them slightly for use on a website as compared to a face to face meeting as well.

Good Luck……

BONUS MATERIAL 2
Step by step formula for successful video marketing

The years 2012 and 2013 were the years of pictures and picture sharing. That's why sites like Pinterest, and Instagram gained huge popularities online in a short amount of time.

My prediction is that 2014 will be the age of video marketing. We see more and more companies representing themselves and their products on video instead of written language. In fact people are 3 times more likely to click on a link with a video than without one.

To become an early adaptor of this trend, it's vital to know the basic principles of video marketing. When creating content for our clients we focus on these five keys principles, and we'd love to be sharing them with you;

1.) **Your video should include testimonials:** There is no better way to market your services than having your patients do it for you.

    Sharing success stories, before and after images, having them share what problem they were having before and how you helped them solve it is a method of "soft-selling" instead of you bragging about how good you are.

2.) **Your videos should be concise and to the point:** People are 5 times less likely to click on a video that's 8 minutes long than a 2 minutes long one. Speed and good content is everything.

3.) **Your video should identify, acknowledge a problem that your client has or he thinks he does.**

4.) **Your video should offer a step by step solution to the problem identified.**

5.) **Your video should convey a convincing message and a promise to have that problem solved.**

There are many sub steps within each of the above to get the best video content out, and we will keep them for another book..

I hope this helps you

BONUS MATERIAL 3

Fail proof guide to determine your ideal and most profitable patient

The goal of this guide is to help you find patients who will appreciate what you do for them, and will be willing to invest a premium amount to get those services. As mentioned in the book, your goal should not be to attract every single living soul to your practice. And by pinpointing exactly whom you would like to offer your services will give you power to eliminate the tire kickers automatically.

By filling in the list and answering the questions, you will find out who your marketing efforts should focus on to get the best results, and be able to work with patients that you enjoy serving.

Your Ideal Client Finder;

1.) **Overall groups:** ex: patients who are prune to having a heart attack, individuals who are looking for plastic surgery, people who need implant treatment. Etc.

2.) **Gender:**

3.) **Education:**

4.) **Profession:**

5.) **Income:** You would like to target people who are capable of paying you for your services based on your average sale. Ex; if you are a plastic surgeon whose average sale is $45000, you should be marketing to patients who make on average 6-10 times more than what you charge.

6.) **Geographic Location:**

7.) **Family and Lifestyle:** Ex: married, with 2 kids, single.

8.) **Online activity:** How does this person spend her time when she is online? What topics get her interest? What websites does she visit frequently?

9.) **Authority or Trust Figures:** Ex: celebrities, politicians, historical figures, role models.

10.) **If she had a magic wand to fix 3 things in her life, what would**

those be related to your field? Ex: lose 15 pounds, start working out, get whiter teeth etc.

11.) **What is her single biggest fear?** Ex: not be able to walk again, lose her sight, become unattractive to her husband, loser hair etc.

12.) **What must she believe about you and your service to buy from you or to choose your practice?** Ex: Trustworthy, caring, capable of solving the problem she's having, good listener etc.

13.) **Name your ideal client:**

If you take a couple of minutes and put a lot of thought through this page while filling in, this will help you make your marketing decision based on this person instead of trying to convert everyone to your patient.

P.O. Box 502

Portland, PA 18351

Oguz.konar@gmail.com

THANK YOU

www.ingramcontent.com/pod-product-compliance
Lightning Source LLC
Chambersburg PA
CBHW071618170526
45166CB00003B/1106